50

REVIEWS FROM READERS

I recently downloaded a couple of books from this series to read over the weekend thinking I would read just one or two. However, I so loved the books that I read all the six books I had downloaded in one go and ended up downloading a few more today. Written by different authors, the books offer practical advice on how you can perform or achieve certain goals in life, which in this case is how to have a better life.

The information is simple to digest and learn from, and is incredibly useful. There are also resources listed at the end of the book that you can use to get more information.

50 Things To Know To Have A Better Life: Self-Improvement Made Easy!

Author Dannii Cohen

This book is very helpful and provides simple tips on how to improve your everyday life. I found it to be useful in improving my overall attitude.

50 Things to Know For Your Mindfulness & Meditation Journey
Author Nina Edmondso

Quick read with 50 short and easy tips for what to think about before starting to homeschool.

50 Things to Know About Getting Started with Homeschool by Author Amanda Walton

I really enjoyed the voice of the narrator, she speaks in a soothing tone. The book is a really great reminder of things we might have known we could do during stressful times, but forgot over the years.

Author Harmony Hawaii

There is so much waste in our society today. Everyone should be forced to read this book. I know I am passing it on to my family.

50 Things to Know to Downsize Your Life: How To Downsize, Organize, And Get Back to Basics

Author Lisa Rusczyk Ed. D.

Great book to get you motivated and understand why you may be losing motivation. Great for that person who wants to start getting healthy, or just for you when you need motivation while having an established workout routine.

50 Things To Know To Stick With A Workout: Motivational Tips To Start The New You Today

Author Sarah Hughes

50 THINGS TO KNOW ABOUT BEING AN ELEMENTARY SCHOOL TEACHER

Lessons Taught Through Experience

McKenna Johnsen

50 Things to Know About Being an Elementary School Teacher   Copyright © 2021 by CZYK Publishing LLC. All Rights Reserved.

All rights reserved. No part of this book may be reproduced in any form or by any electronic or mechanical means including information storage and retrieval systems, without permission in writing from the author. The only exception is by a reviewer, who may quote short excerpts in a review.
The statements in this book are of the authors and may not be the views of CZYK Publishing or 50 Things to Know.

Cover designed by: Ivana Stamenkovic
Cover Image: https://pixabay.com/photos/teacher-property-plant-and-teaching-3765909/

CZYK Publishing Since 2011.
CZYKPublishing.com
50 Things to Know

Lock Haven, PA
All rights reserved.
ISBN: 9798702425245

50 THINGS TO KNOW ABOUT BEING AN ELEMENTARY SCHOOL TEACHER

BOOK DESCRIPTION

Are you interested in becoming an elementary teacher? Do you have a desire to make a difference in the lives of hundreds of children? Would you like to know the honest truth about what daily life looks like as an educator? If you answered yes to any of these questions then this book is for you... 50 Things to Know About Being an Elementary Teacher by author McKenna Johnsen offers an approach to the secrets behind elementary teaching. Most books on being a teacher tell you to pursue the career because of the positive aspects such as getting to work with kids all day, or having summer months off. Although there's nothing wrong with that, before pursuing an elementary teaching license you also need to examine the field through the honest lens of a public school teacher, and determine for yourself whether a teaching career is the best fit for you. Based on knowledge from the world's leading experts the field of elementary education is expected to grow 4% over the next 10 years, which means now may be the perfect time for you to dip your toes into the life of a teacher. In these pages you'll discover what the lifestyle of an elementary teacher looks like both in the classroom and beyond. This book will help you determine whether being an elementary educator is the ideal career for you. By the time you finish this book, you will know both the challenges and highlights of classroom teaching across a variety of environments. So grab YOUR copy today. You'll be glad you did.

TABLE OF CONTENTS

50 Things to Know
Book Series
Reviews from Readers
50 Things to Know About Being an Elementary School Teacher
BOOK DESCRIPTION
TABLE OF CONTENTS
DEDICATION
ABOUT THE AUTHOR
INTRODUCTION
1. Every Day is Different
2. Students Become Second Family
3. Kids Observe Every Move
4. Accomplishing Walking Goals is Easy
5. Having a Teacher Face is Key
6. Kids are Funny
7. Work Days May be Long
8. Teachers Wear Many Hats
9. There are Many Teaching Environments
10. Elementary Teachers Have Fun
11. Teaching is a Full-Time Acting Gig
12. Elementary Teachers Act Like Students
13. Teachers Learn From Students

14. Student Accomplishments Make Teachers Feel Prideful
15. Teachers Fight for Their Students
16. Creativity is Essential
17. Teaching is Exhausting
18. Teachers Get Blamed
19. The Diet Matches the Child
20. Teachers Go Above and Beyond
21. Elementary Teachers Adapt on the Fly
23. Expect the Unexpected
24. Teachers Do Strange Things
25. Parents Challenge You
26. Elementary Teachers Make Great Lie Detectors
27. Teachers Spend All Day Talking With Children
28. Teachers Cry
29. Silliness Makes Everything Better
30. Elementary Teachers Deserve Long Breaks
31. Maintaining a Work-Life Balance is Essential
32. Lesson Planning is All About Borrowing
33. Data is a Teacher's Best Friend
34. Elementary Teachers Love School Supplies
35. Students Adore You
36. Teachers Rarely Take Breaks
37. Many Tasks are Not in the Original Job Description
38. The Party is in the Staff Room

39. Every District is Unique
40. The Salary Allows for a Comfortable Life
41. Be Careful About Social Media
42. Report Cards are About the Parents
43. Holidays Get Controversial
44. The Week Before a Break Brings New Challenges
45. Losing Teeth Becomes a Daily Occurance
46. The First Week is Not Reality
47. Equity is Always on the Mind
48. Students are all Special
49. Teaching is Great Parent Training
50. Elementary Teachers Teach With Their Heart

Other Resources:

50 Things to Know

DEDICATION

This book is dedicated to the incredible teachers that support me each and every day: Mary, Diane, Brooke, Tiffany, and my wonderful mom, Laurie.

ABOUT THE AUTHOR

McKenna Johnsen is an elementary educator from Portland, Oregon. Throughout her career as a teacher, McKenna has worked in a variety of school settings, including public, private, and charter schools. She has experience teaching both in the classroom and online, giving readers a unique perspective into all of the potential teaching environments one might pursue. In addition to teaching, McKenna received her Masters in Education along with an ESOL endorsement from California Lutheran University. She is currently working as a first grade teacher in the Portland area.

In her free time, McKenna loves to spend time exploring the beautiful Pacific Northwest with her friends and family. She also loves running, traveling, and the occasional nap. To learn more about McKenna Johnsen, you can check out her Instagram account at mckennajohnsen.

INTRODUCTION

"Teaching seems to require the sort of skills one would need to pilot a bus full of live chickens backwards, with no brakes, down a rocky road through the Andes while providing colorful and informative commentary on the scenery."

-Franklin Habit

We have all been impacted by teachers. There were some that taught us to read and write, others that showed us the importance of working hard, and teachers who taught us that it is okay to be imperfect as long as we try our best. There is no denying that becoming an elementary teacher gives you the ability to change lives in many different ways. With that said, the profession also comes with its own set of everyday challenges. I hope that you use the perspectives stated in this book to form your own opinions about elementary teaching. Perhaps this will even be the first step towards a long and rewarding career in the field. Let the truth begin!

1. EVERY DAY IS DIFFERENT

As an elementary teacher, I wake up everyday thinking "I wonder what adventure today will bring". No matter how much I prepare and plan each lesson in depth, something is bound to change your teaching plans. Perhaps drama will unfold at recess and your upcoming math lesson suddenly needs to become a restorative justice circle. Maybe a student will instantaneously feel over-stimulated, run circles around your classroom, and throw hundreds of your neatly organized books around the room, thus causing an emergency classroom evacuation. On the bright side, some days you have a spontaneous guest speaker dressed up in a silly costume stop by for a visit. There could even be a last minute celebration assembly that takes place, allowing you to spend your afternoon singing and dancing along with your students. Then some days everything goes exactly according to plan and you feel thrilled by the outcome. These are all scenarios that have happened during my years as an elementary teacher. Every day is special, and as a teacher you learn to embrace and welcome whatever may be thrown your way.

2. STUDENTS BECOME SECOND FAMILY

This lesson I learned the hard way. I was 22 years old and on a date. During the date, I kept talking about "my kids". I explained all of the exciting things they were up to at school, the progress they were making in reading, and the fun games we have played together. It was not until halfway through the evening when I realized that my date thought I had actual kids of my own. At that point I had to explain to him that the entire time I had been referring to my students. From that moment on it became clear to me that my students truly are like family. I often talk about them as though they are my own, which confuses many who are not in the profession. With that said, it warms my heart to brag about my students and their accomplishments. I love to talk about their strengths, activities we do together, and the silly conversations students and I have on a daily basis. We laugh together, cry together, celebrate together, and have each other's backs. Students are my family, and if you enter the teaching profession, your future students will most-likely feel like family to you too.

3. KIDS OBSERVE EVERY MOVE

If you are a parent, this tip may come as no surprise to you. Kids are some of the most observant beings on this planet. Everything you do and say will be internalized by our future generations. This may sound scary, but as a teacher, knowing this fact makes you feel incredibly powerful. As an elementary teacher, you need to be aware that your actions are being seen, and your words are being heard. Books you read and videos you show will be soaked into each child like a sponge, for better or for worse.

I remember in my student teaching days, I worked with a teacher that always said "my goodness, doggy!" when something went wrong. Then all of a sudden, we noticed students start to imitate and say "my goodness, doggy!" when they made a mistake.

Many students will imitate without realizing it. This often feels rewarding when a student begins to say phrases like "I love making mistakes" or "I can do this"! At times you may catch students imitating the Big, Bad Wolf after reading Little Red Riding Hood or acting like a sword-fighting ninja they saw on television the night before. Needless to say, kids are watching, and they are listening. As a teacher, you must take this to heart and think twice about your every move.

4. ACCOMPLISHING WALKING GOALS IS EASY

I remember one year when I was teaching second grade. Students and I had contests to see which of us could get the most steps in a day, which we tracked on our watches. Though this began as motivation for students and I to stay active during the school day, it made me realize just how many steps teachers get without putting in extra effort. As an elementary teacher, you spend the entire day on your feet. Some days I will not sit down from the day work begins, around 7:30, until 3:15 when my students have officially left for the day. I spend my time walking around the classroom to check on students, work with groups, or to distribute supplies.

As a primary teacher, students often have short attention spans, so we change activities every 20 minutes. This typically means we need to change locations in order to feel engaged. I walk students to and from their elective classes, recess, the lunch room, and assemblies. If I need to make copies or grab some extra school supplies I walk to the work room. When it is lunch time I walk to the staff lounge. Then there are the days when I have recess duty and spend 20 minutes running races with students or climbing around on the monkey bars with them. Although that last part is not a requirement for being an elementary teacher, the moral of the story is that teachers get their steps. We are constantly on the move whether we intend for it to happen or not. But hey, it keeps our heart healthy and our minds awake, right?

5. HAVING A TEACHER FACE IS KEY

If a student is not behaving, the best teachers have a special look. That look means everything. As an elementary teacher, kids should be able to tell their teacher's emotions by a quick examination of their face. When I am happy, my students know it, and they smile with me. If I feel upset, students will ask what is on my mind. For the moments when I feel angry with a student, that student will hunch down and know they did something wrong. The "teacher face" is unique to each educator, but expressing your emotions through your facial features will alter the attitudes of your students. At times this means that teachers need to mask their emotions in order to protect children and make them feel comfortable and safe in the classroom. At other times, it is okay to let your vulnerable and honest "teacher face" show, so long as it is followed by a discussion on why you are feeling upset. Kids like when you are honest. Just remember that whatever shows on your "teacher face" will be observed and interpreted by students.

Managing your emotions with those special teacher looks are key.

6. KIDS ARE FUNNY

In the previous tip, I mentioned that students are good at reading your "teacher face". When kids are hilarious, yet they are saying or doing something inappropriate, this is when your "teacher face" truly gets put to the test. Sometimes students make political jokes about the current president at the time, and no matter how funny it may seem, you have to maintain your best "teacher face" and try to keep a neutral perspective.

But the reality of it is, kids are funny. Most of the time they do not realize their own wonderful sense of humor. As a teacher, students make me laugh constantly. In fact, each year I keep a journal of the funniest quotes said by my students for my own personal enjoyment. One year I wrote down over 40 funny sayings said by my kiddos. I hear students say cute things like "when I grow up, I want to be a superhero!". When asked about their weekends, I've had a student say "instead of going to sleep, I had a party in my closet!" When learning about solar power, a student once stated in a concerned voice, "is the sun going to get smaller from all the solar panels taking it?" The innocence of a child has the opportunity to bring joy unlike any other. As a teacher, be ready to laugh and smile until your belly hurts and your cheeks get sore. Just don't forget about that tricky "teacher face".

7. WORK DAYS MAY BE LONG

Teachers are some of the hardest workers you will meet. Some may think of a teacher as working only when students are in school, from around 8 to 3. This is entirely untrue. As a teacher, not only do we work our full 8 hour shifts along with the rest of the working force, but we also work nights, weekends, and during our breaks. During my first years of teaching, I would get to work 90 minutes early, and stay an hour after each day working on lesson plans, analyzing student data, catching up on emails, or prepping materials for the next day. Though it is possible to take weekends off from work and relax in the evenings, as an educator I guarantee that there will be days when you simply have to work more than you had hoped. Teachers need professional development hours, we take classes, and there are many meetings with parents and other faculty that limit the amount of time we have during the work day to focus on the highlight of our job; the actual teaching of our students. With that said, as you grow in experience your workload will ease up and you will be able to maintain a more balanced life. As with any profession, if you want to excel in your career, you have to put in the time and effort. If you work hard and try your best as a teacher, there is no doubt that you will be able to feel accomplished and make a difference for hundreds of children.

8. TEACHERS WEAR MANY HATS

Though our title technically says "teacher", there are many other hats that us in education wear on a daily basis. For example, imagine that a child rushes to you with a bloody knee from falling down at recess. At that point you turn into the nurse and help get the child a bandaid. Then, later in the day, a student gets into an argument with another student while playing a math game. As the teacher, you become the school therapist by mediating the situation and get both children feeling happy with one another again. After that, a student comes to you with a shoe untied. "Mommy please tie my shoe!" the kid asks. You kindly remind the child that you are their teacher, not their mom, but proceed to tie their shoe. With that said, the role of being a parent to 25 young children definitely is a hat worn by all teachers during the school day. Though our job description says that we are expected to teach children, our various hats show that teachers are much more than that. We are the nurses, the therapists, the parents, and sometimes the friend. As a teacher you must love children enough to embrace all those different roles.

9. THERE ARE MANY TEACHING ENVIRONMENTS

I have experience teaching in 4 very different environments. Each environment has their own perks. Throughout my initial days of teaching, I spent a great deal of time in a private school environment. Here the class sizes are often small. Students may have similar interests or ideologies. Teachers in private school have unique experiences that may not be allowed in other settings, which can make the learning fun. Private schools often have a focus such as Christianity or the arts. I also have taught in a charter school, which is essentially a free private school. At charter schools, teachers often get more freedom in what they teach and how they teach core subjects. Charter schools may even have a focus such as "STEM" or "project based learning". Teaching in this environment was a bit more demanding than other schools, in my experience, but the freedom makes it worth the while. From here I switched to teaching in a general public school. Public schools have great support systems. There are always people to work with you in a team and assist with your needs, whether they may be personal or school-related. Public schools often are less predictable, with larger class sizes and students frequently coming and going throughout the year. Lastly, I have worked in an online school. This is the best option if you are looking for a work-life balance. You will be able to work in a casual setting from home, and you never have to worry about morning traffic and commuting.

If you are interested in becoming a teacher without the hassle of classroom management, this might be a great environment for you. Each teaching environment is unique and it is important to take the time to learn about them before committing to a job.

10. ELEMENTARY TEACHERS HAVE FUN

Personally, I love any excuse to celebrate. I enjoy student birthdays, holidays, fridays, and the days when we finish a unit in reading. These are all reasons for students and teachers to come together and get excited about all we have achieved. If you feel excited about something, students frequently follow suit. As a teacher I plan fun events and "parties" at least once a month, but sometimes they occur once a week. Celebrations keep learning fun and enjoyable for all of us in the classroom, and they are a great balance after many days of hard work and dedication to learning a tough curriculum of material.

11. TEACHING IS A FULL-TIME ACTING GIG

Have you ever seen a Disney Princess at Disneyland? That is exactly how I feel as an elementary teacher. My voice is often 5 octaves higher when speaking with young children, my language becomes more simplified, and I almost always talk with a smile on my face. We sing, we dance, we paint together. At times I often feel like I was hired to be an actress rather than a teacher. But just like acting, teaching sometimes feels draining after putting on a face for students all day long. Feeling the need to mask real emotions may also get tiring. With that said, elementary classrooms are filled with positivity, joy and happiness which in turn makes the work day appear shorter and less dull.

12. ELEMENTARY TEACHERS ACT LIKE STUDENTS

Sometimes when students are at recess, I feel the desire to play along with them. On a typical day as an elementary teacher, you will see me swinging on the monkey bars, racing students around the school track, or sliding down the slide at full speed. As an elementary teacher, you cannot be afraid to act like your students sometimes. Obviously there are moments when you need to be mature and professional, but as a teacher, you have the freedom to make life more fun by embracing your inner child. As stated in previous tips, elementary teachers can sing, dance, and make jokes, and that is perfectly alright! Life is too short to be boring.

13. TEACHERS LEARN FROM STUDENTS

Students are like sponges; they soak up information from all different moments in their lives. Although I spend all day teaching them reading, writing, and math, students learn on the playground, in their special classes like PE and music, and while at home or even sports practice. I love when students come to school ready to share new things they have learned. Some students come to me to explain things like how to turn on the farting feature in a Tesla, or the fact that polar bears only live in the North Pole region. It is amazing how many unusual facts I have learned from my students over the years. As a teacher, I love learning which is what led me into the profession, so learning from students makes the classroom exciting, no matter how old you are!

14. STUDENT ACCOMPLISHMENTS MAKE TEACHERS FEEL PRIDEFUL

One year I taught second grade. In class I had a student a few years behind grade level in reading. Over time I could see her confidence diminish and her frustrations growing stronger. After school one day I made an intervention plan for this one specific student. Each day I worked with the student for 45 minutes, during which time we practiced phonics skills, sight words, sentence fluency, and expression while reading. After nearly 4 months of nonstop daily practice, I finally saw this student make huge strides. Her reading started to take off, and the smiles on her face after reading a full page of text truly made it all worth the while. Teachers take pride in their students' accomplishments. It is an exciting moment when students make progress, and teachers deserve some credit when things go well!

15. TEACHERS FIGHT FOR THEIR STUDENTS

It is a fact that teachers spend basically all day, Monday-Friday, surrounded by their students. As a teacher, we know what they eat, their favorite games to play, as well as their strengths and weaknesses. Sometimes teachers know these traits better than the students' own families, especially when it comes to academics. This is why teachers are responsible for fighting for their students.

When a student struggles in a particular subject, teachers fight for them to receive something called an IEP (Individualized Education Plan) or a 504 plan. When a teacher requests that a child be evaluated for one of these plans, it simply means that the child needs some additional support systems in place in order to succeed in the traditional school environment. In this process a student needs to be evaluated, then the teacher will be asked to attend meetings with the child's family as well as a child study team typically consisting of principals, the school counselor, and other teachers. It still amazes me how much schools accomplish when we all put our heads together to fight for a child's success.

16. CREATIVITY IS ESSENTIAL

On March 11, 2020, my school completely shut down due to the COVID-19 virus. During this time, all teachers were forced to work remotely and participate in something my district called distance learning. Everything that I had studied in my Masters program completely got thrown down the drain as my team of teachers and I frantically searched for new and innovative ways to teach children virtually. I researched many websites that made learning fun and interactive. I also held live lessons while teaching online where I would spend time singing, dancing, and connecting with students as much as possible. My creativity was constantly tested, but in the end, I loved school and so did many of my students, despite the chaotic transition to a new way of learning. Creativity is key as an elementary teacher.

17. TEACHING IS EXHAUSTING

It is no secret that teachers work long hours. During those hours, you are constantly on your feet, moving from place to place. Physically, you feel drained at the end of the day. While you get your daily step count in, your mental health is also frequently tested. Students may not always behave, and you will spend time speaking with individual students and managing an entire class. That classroom management piece is sometimes purely exhausting. To prevent teacher burnout, you must try to incorporate relaxation and calm in your everyday routines to balance the stress of teaching. Though you may frequently end the day feeling tired, hopefully the knowledge of knowing you tried your best and made a difference for your students makes it all worth it.

18. TEACHERS GET BLAMED

If a child is not making sufficient progress academically, there is a chance that the teacher will get blamed. Then when a child gets called a name on the playground, the teacher may get blamed for not stepping in sooner. Needless to say, there is always a chance of teachers getting blamed for just about anything. It is part of the job and bound to happen, so as an educator you need to learn how to take ownership for your actions when necessary and act with confidence and kindness when addressing these negative situations.

19. THE DIET MATCHES THE CHILD

This tip is hilarious, yet incredibly true for many teachers. As a teacher, I notice my routines and diet changing during the school year. For example, I eat a snack at 10:10 everyday, because in the classroom this is when students have snack time. I crave lunch at precisely 11:40, and need another snack right at the end of the day, as do my students. Even when away from school I found myself cooking foods that my students loved, such as chicken nuggets, macaroni and cheese, and Goldfish crackers. Although I am a full grown adult, it is funny how much the foods of my students influence my personal diet.

20. TEACHERS GO ABOVE AND BEYOND

An elementary teacher's goal is to ensure that students feel successful academically, socially, and emotionally. Sometimes this means that we need to put in additional effort to make this happen. Teachers might work with students before or after school. We differentiate often, meaning we create assignments and projects for specific students depending on their needs and abilities. Oftentimes a little extra effort will go a long way to make a student feel successful at school.

21. ELEMENTARY TEACHERS ADAPT ON THE FLY

As a teacher, we often have to switch our plans at the drop of a hat. In elementary school, this is often driven by student behavior. When students behave well, you might change your daily agenda to include more games, art, and fun. On days where students are struggling with behavior, sometimes teachers have to adapt their plans to include calming activities like reading, writing, or building silently with Playdoh. Having the ability to adapt is essential as an elementary teacher because students are frequently unpredictable and impulsive. This is simply their stage of development, so we as teachers must change our plans to meet the needs of everyone.

22. EVERY TEACHER IS UNIQUE

Personally, I am an elementary teacher full of energy. In my class, students are singing, dancing, and playing games to learn the curriculum. With that said, every teacher is unique and has their own preferences. Some need structure and routines, while others are more flexible. There are teachers that like to keep the classroom calm, and others that want their room to feel energized. Teachers like whole-group instruction, while some prefer students to work in small groups or individually. If a teacher feels passionate about a particular topic, they are more likely to spend time creating thorough and educational lessons related to the subject. Each educator has their own style, which is what makes learning fresh and fun for students!

23. EXPECT THE UNEXPECTED

One minute a child might throw themselves on the ground screaming because they lost a marker, then the next minute a smiley kid will run up to you with a tooth in their hand because they just pulled it out of their mouth while you were instructing. In short, expect the unexpected. Lessons may move slower or faster than expected, and that is okay. Teachers do their best to teach the curriculum, while understanding that things may suddenly not go according to the plan. Sometimes they turn out even better.

24. TEACHERS DO STRANGE THINGS

At the last school I taught at, the classrooms all had windows so that teachers could see what other teachers were doing in class. While walking through the halls, I realized just how special and silly teachers could be during lessons. I saw teachers doing yoga with students, stomping around like an elephant, singing, dancing, or chanting. Teachers do strange things to help students remember material. It works, but it does make us look silly at times. As a teacher, you simply need to take hold of your confidence and roll with it.

25. PARENTS CHALLENGE YOU

Parents are protective of their children, and understandably so. When their child comes home from school crying because of an incident at recess or a bullying situation, parents frequently go straight to the teacher for help. Sometimes parents believe their child needs to be pushed more in reading, or get some additional support with writing. They fight for their kid, and teachers are on the frontline to address each challenge thrown our way. Although the teacher nor the parent are always right, it is an important part of our job to work with families to create mutual agreements and understandings based on what is best for each child. Though parent meetings can at times be stressful, they are what better us as educators and help our future generations most.

26. ELEMENTARY TEACHERS MAKE GREAT LIE DETECTORS

Fortunately for us, children are not always the best at lying. I find this to be the most true on the playground. Students often come up to you with a "he said, she said" scenario. As a teacher, your task is to sit children down and get to the bottom of each situation until it is resolved. Conflict resolution and encouraging students to tell the truth is what helps teach children to be responsible, kind, and accountable.

27. TEACHERS SPEND ALL DAY TALKING WITH CHILDREN

This concept has gotten me into trouble several times. All day long I address students as "friends" and use very simple language to get my points across. While this is helpful for students, speaking in child-friendly language is not helpful when speaking with adults. Sometimes I find myself speaking to my friends and family with phrases like "you are such a silly goose" and they look at me like I am crazy. Frequently I do not even realize that I talk in this positive, simple way. It is the price you pay to be a teacher!

28. TEACHERS CRY

Speaking of the "price you pay to be a teacher", it is important to note that teachers sometimes have bad days. Typically your mood is related to classroom management difficulties. I can remember one day going to my principal at the end of the day and just sobbing because I felt so frustrated by a particular situation that occurred earlier. She reassured me that everything would be okay, and eventually I calmed down and moved on with my agenda. Though teachers are strong most days, just like everyone else, we are only human, and sometimes that means we cry too.

29. SILLINESS MAKES EVERYTHING BETTER

Life is short. Having fun makes any job worthwhile, and teaching is no exception. In the classroom, teachers want to laugh, smile, be silly, and have a good time along with their students. As a teacher we have the freedom to make our job as enjoyable as we want. Some days, I just want to dance, so I tell my class to stand up and we dance. Other days I want to read books like "Creepy Pair of Underwear" to make me smile, so that is what we do. If you focus too much on the curriculum and teaching to the text, students will not enjoy learning. On the other hand, if students love learning and you love teaching in silly ways, life will be better and children will remember your lessons.

30. ELEMENTARY TEACHERS DESERVE LONG BREAKS

After working long hours every week, often including nights and weekends, it is no secret that teachers deserve their breaks. We have Winter Break, Spring Break, and often a week at Thanksgiving. During these breaks teachers have the chance to relax, spend time with loved ones, and catch up on the things they have been meaning to do for the months while they were teaching but felt too busy to do them. These breaks allow us to live a balanced life. In the summers I love to travel, and during other breaks I love to go on adventures. These breaks are well deserved after all of the hard work teachers put in throughout the school year.

31. MAINTAINING A WORK-LIFE BALANCE IS ESSENTIAL

This is a tip that I cannot stress enough. As an educator, there is always more work that could be done. The best thing you can do for your mental and emotional health is to close the planning books at a specific time everyday and go home. For me, I began my teaching career working from 7:30 until 5:00 everyday, then I would spend my nights and weekends with more grading and planning. This made me feel extremely burnt out and exhausted by the end of the year. When the next school year rolled around, I forced myself to go home right at 3:30, the end of my contract hours, almost every day. I tried not to work on nights and weekends and this improved my mental health immensely. I highly recommend striving for a work-life balance.

32. LESSON PLANNING IS ALL ABOUT BORROWING

When you first get hired as an elementary teacher, you will most likely be given curriculum books to teach from. These books tell you what to teach, and how to teach it. For those that want to spice up their lessons, they often turn to other teachers for ideas, or find fun and engaging lessons on the internet. Teachers do not need to come up with everything on their own. We are a team and are there to support one another with our lesson ideas!

33. DATA IS A TEACHER'S BEST FRIEND

Whenever you are meeting with the administration team or the families of your students, you want to be ready to back up all of your claims with data. If a student is struggling with reading, you want to be ready with the child's exact reading level, sight word knowledge, phonics strengths, etc. The more data you collect on each child, the more other people will be confident in your abilities and knowledge. Personally, I kept a journal of student data and tried to meet with each student at least once a week individually to assess their academic abilities. Data will be your best friend as a teacher.

34. ELEMENTARY TEACHERS LOVE SCHOOL SUPPLIES

You know that giddy feeling you got as a child when you received a gift you had been dreaming about for months on end? That is essentially how teachers feel about a brand new batch of school supplies. These supplies will make everyday life in the classroom easier. From new notebooks, to drawing paper, to rulers and art kits, the more supplies a classroom has, the more opportunities you all will have to learn. Supplies often go missing, break, or wear out, so having an abundance of supplies available throughout the year really makes a positive impact on teachers and students alike.

35. STUDENTS ADORE YOU

As an elementary teacher, nothing warms your heart more than when a student does something sweet for you. They might draw you a pretty picture, write a note, or do a random act of kindness to make you happy. Students adore their teachers and often love to bring them joy. These little moments of reassurance are what make the profession of teaching feel worth it.

36. TEACHERS RARELY TAKE BREAKS

Breaks are for preparation. During recess, specials, and lunch time, teachers often are prepping materials, lesson planning, or responding to emails. We are on our feet moving around the building, and rarely get the chance to sit and focus on something other than work. I often tried to sit and eat lunch for at least 20 minutes every day. During this time I talked with my coworkers about anything other than school, which made the day feel less stressful. With that said, breaks are not often as a teacher, so you really do just have to love what you do in the profession.

37. MANY TASKS ARE NOT IN THE ORIGINAL JOB DESCRIPTION

Two years ago, I remember we had a school assembly with over 500 students and families watching. The staff decided to surprise students with a choreographed dance. When it was my part, I was the teacher that did cartwheels down the center aisle, wearing a penguin onesie costume and pigtails. Did I mention that there were 500 families watching? Many things that teachers are asked to do are not in our original job description, but we do them anyways because they make others happy.

38. THE PARTY IS IN THE STAFF ROOM

On days when I was feeling tired or down, I always made sure to stop by the staff room during my breaks. In the staff room I often found delicious treats donated by other staff members, students, or the community. My favorite days were when we had donuts or homemade brownies. The staff room also raised my spirits because it was the one place in the building where I could talk to staff members about anything, away from the chaos of teaching. We laughed while talking about the latest movies we watched, I learned about my coworker and her hundred chickens she was raising, and I caught them all up on the joys of being a young millennial teacher. The staff room is where teachers often go to laugh, relax, and have some fun throughout their days.

39. EVERY DISTRICT IS UNIQUE

Throughout my career I have taught in 3 completely different teaching environments. One school was focused on project based learning, and students spent time studying extra-curricular activities like languages or the arts. Another school was focused on equity and inclusion, and we taught social-emotional skills regularly. Currently I work as a virtual teacher, so my main goal is to create engaging and fun lessons more than anything. Every district is unique and it is important to do your research before accepting any position.

40. THE SALARY ALLOWS FOR A COMFORTABLE LIFE

I was raised in a family of teachers. My parents were teachers, grandparents were teachers, aunts and uncles were all teachers. As an expert in the life of a teacher, I find it important to point out that although the salary of teachers is often criticized for being low, working in education does allow for a comfortable life if you know how to save money. Growing up, my family and I went on road trips every summer. We went on vacations, had plenty of toys and technology, as well as a nice house to live in. Do not fear teaching because of the salary. Save wisely and you too will be able to live an enjoyable life with plenty of nice things.

41. BE CAREFUL ABOUT SOCIAL MEDIA

Teachers are one of the most sued professions. With this in mind, it is important that you keep your social media private. Never post pictures that include students, families, or details about work. You can face significant legal action if you choose to post these kinds of words or pictures. Overall, just be careful what you post online, because it is public. The last thing a teacher wants is more added stress to their personal life on top of their already busy profession.

42. REPORT CARDS ARE ABOUT THE PARENTS

A first grader does not care if they have perfect grades. Oftentimes they just want to know that they are learning and on track academically. Report cards in elementary school are all about the parents. Parents want to know how their child is performing because they want them to succeed. As a teacher, I always include report card comments that are both personalized and positive. Never do I want parents to feel that their child is a failure. Every student has great qualities. Even though some may be struggling in a particular subject area, as a teacher, report cards are a great time to communicate in positive and effective ways to all of your families. Make sure that parents know that their child is loved, and being educated in the best ways possible. Parents also should know that no child is perfect.

43. HOLIDAYS GET CONTROVERSIAL

This tip has become more evident in recent years. As a child, we always had big Halloween costume parades, Christmas parties, and Valentine's celebrations. These days, schools have changed their stance to be more inclusive. That means that most districts do not want you to celebrate a holiday, especially if it is religious-based such as Christmas. Instead, holidays are replaced with seasonal celebrations like a "Winter Party" or "Friendship Day" instead of Valentine's Day. Holidays are slowly becoming a thing of the past, and it is happening with the intention of making schools more inclusive of students from all places and backgrounds.

44. THE WEEK BEFORE A BREAK BRINGS NEW CHALLENGES

The week before Winter Break, teachers often try to hide the fact that students are about to get 2 full weeks off from school. More than ever, we try to maintain structure as much as possible, despite the parties, assemblies, and celebratory activities that may be taking place that week. Classroom management gets harder because students are focused on the fun weeks ahead. Many are heading on vacations. Some will get to see family they have not seen in a long time. It is hard for students, and teachers alike, to focus on academics. So instead, plan for this week to be structured, yet relaxed. I tend to do everything in my power to keep students calm, focused, and busy. The week before breaks brings challenges, but can also be filled with fun. It is all about balance.

45. LOSING TEETH BECOMES A DAILY OCCURANCE

This is particularly true in the younger grades. The other day I had a student raise their hand to say that they lost their front tooth. They then proceeded to smile a beautiful, toothless smile, which warmed my heart. These days remind me of the innocence and youthfulness of children. With that said, once a student says they lost a tooth, every child in the class wants to share their tooth story. They want to tell you how many wiggly teeth they have, and they want to explain in depth what happens at home when they lose a tooth. Then the topic of the tooth fairy will come up, which often becomes controversial. As a teacher, mentally prepare for teeth losing. Have ways to celebrate when students lose teeth, have ways for them to save their teeth to take home, and also be ready to address these situations to prevent a half hour detour from lessons that will instead become a full blown discussion about losing teeth.

46. THE FIRST WEEK IS NOT REALITY

When students show up on the first day of school, they are not yet comfortable. They might feel nervous, sad, or conflicted. This causes them to behave in mostly angelic ways for the first few days until they become comfortable with their teacher and classmates. Then, before too long, one student will test their boundaries. They might say something inappropriate, or do something against your class rules to see what happens. During the first week of school it is essential that you spend time reinforcing rules. If you allow a child to get away with something, before long your room will turn to chaos. The first week of school teachers always do their best to get structures, routines and policies solidified to make for an easier and more enjoyable school year.

47. EQUITY IS ALWAYS ON THE MIND

Similar to the rest of the world, equity has changed the way we look at everyday life. As a teacher, you constantly think about your specific population of students. Where are they from? What is their socio-economic status? What do they enjoy? All of these factors will be used to frame your lessons as a teacher. This holds true when teachers develop test questions, plan assignments, or create fun activities. Equity is always on our minds so that we are inclusive of students from all backgrounds.

48. STUDENTS ARE ALL SPECIAL

As a teacher, I fall in love with the qualities of all of my students. Some make me smile with their jokes, others impress me with their attention to detail on school assignments. Each child has strengths, and as a teacher it is our duty to bring these strengths out of them and build their confidence as individuals.

49. TEACHING IS GREAT PARENT TRAINING

As a young teacher without kids, I have learned so many things about parenting. I have learned about the different attention spans for children, what they enjoy doing, and how to best manage them when their emotions are frequently varying. All of these skills will be great as I enter the stage of motherhood one day. I will better be able to help my future children emotionally, socially, physically, as well as academically. Teaching is great if you ever want to become a parent!

50. ELEMENTARY TEACHERS TEACH WITH THEIR HEART

All in all, elementary teachers want to make a difference. They hope to shape future generations of students and impact them in a variety of positive ways. To be a teacher, you need to have a big heart. You must be ready to take all of the tips in this book to heart, and in return you will change the world. After learning all of the strengths and challenges of this career, if you feel called to be a leader in your community and make a difference in the lives of hundreds of children, then becoming an elementary teacher is the right field for you. I wish you the best of luck in all your future endeavors.

OTHER RESOURCES:

Occupational Outlook Handbook:
https://www.bls.gov/ooh/education-training-and-library/kindergarten-and-elementary-school-teachers.htm#tab-6

Teachers Pay Teachers:
https://www.teacherspayteachers.com/

Newsela:
https://newsela.com/

READ OTHER 50 THINGS TO KNOW BOOKS

50 Things to Know About Coping With Stress: By A Mental Health Specialist by Kimberly L. Brownridge

50 Things to Know About Being a Zookeeper: Life of a Zookeeper by Stephanie Fowlie

50 Things to Know About Becoming a Doctor: The Journey from Medical School of the Medical Profession by Tong Liu MD

50 Things to Know About Knitting: Knit, Purl, Tricks & Shortcuts by Christina Fanelli

50 Things to Know

Stay up to date with new releases on Amazon:
https://amzn.to/2VPNGr7

CZYKPublishing.com

50 Things to Know

We'd love to hear what you think about our content! Please leave your honest review of this book on Amazon and Goodreads. We appreciate your positive and constructive feedback. Thank you.

Made in the USA
Columbia, SC
19 November 2021